God, War, and California

S.L. Schmidt

BookLeaf Publishing

Presentation by *BookLeaf Publishing*

Web: www.bookleafpub.com

E-mail: info@bookleafpub.com

ISBN: 978-93-95950-40-4

First edition 2022

These poems are dedicated to the friends, family, and strangers with whom I have the pleasure of sharing my brief moment of time alive in this Universe with.

ACKNOWLEDGEMENT

For my Parents,
Sisters,
Brothers,
And above all,
The Family I found in my Friends.

PREFACE

I've heard that poetry is about finding the extraordinary in the mundane. I can't say I agree with that sentiment- to do so would disparage the simple beauty and wonders of being alive.

Life is extraordinary. Living is an extraordinary experience.

I don't believe that anything in this life is mundane.

That being said, many of my poems focus on sensational subjects like war and violence, but it is not the image of active battlefields that make these events seem extraordinary to me. It is how they reflect the human condition.

The following verses detailing cataclysmic war and my more simplistic, "slice-of-life" poems serve the same purpose: to reflect the deep universal experiences of human longing, loneliness, rage, and wonderment.

The human experience is extraordinary, from the darkest depths of our capacity for evil to the way seeing smoke spiral in the air can make us feel alive.

Again and Again

A holy war is won
Weary bodies of our young
Stomp over ash and broken glass
Choking on smog from the still smoking gun

Men will fight,
Men will kill,
Men will bleed,

While a woman under aim of barrel
Hides her face behind her hair and pleads
With a scream: “Don’t make that decision for
me!”

Her prayers for peace again neglected,
A timeless history again repeated;
Greed satisfied at the price of innocent life-
A child mourns their mother

As men again march off to fight.

Blood God

Crimson stained alters
A masquerade of martyrs
Prayer that preaches sin-
What unholy faith is this?

A void of violent voices,
Who can hope to make a sound here?
We've tried to hear the gospel,
But the gunfire is louder.

Blood on the pavement
Outside their Church
Blood in the pages
They Worship

Blood in their motives
Blood in their plans
Blood in their veins,
Blood on their hands.

Blue High Rise

There's a high rise downtown that overlooks the
sea.
When I first saw that blue building, from inside
on the 20th story,
Your presence was a storm cloud brewing over
me.

When I last saw the high rise downtown that
overlooks the sea,
It was from outside, basked in purple flood
lights
In the company of a crowd screaming for a band
you never liked,

I danced because I felt so free without you there
to rain on me.

California

In the city from a postcard
All glossy rooftops and crystal nights,
I’m gleamed in green by the city lights in the skyline
Because I could never make anyone feel as alive as they do.

Canvas

Were my life a canvas,
What I've lived a painting,
Then it would be empty
For vibrant color waiting;

Through these youthful eyes
So little have I seen
A portrait of my life
Would show as incomplete

But still potential waits-
Enclosed in pores of blank white space

A palette full with time that I still have;
I'll dab on pink for every time I laugh
A splash of burning red for bursts of strife-
This mess of hues to light the landscape of my
life

White will fade away
Radiance will spill
The colors of life cascade-
Watch a canvas fill!

Chess

If this game is in our nature
Why must Bishops lead us in prayer when the board is set?
If this lust is in our blood
Why do we retch when red spills across the checkered mat?

Pieces dance around the board again
Till all the Pawns and Rooks fall dead
Departed Knights tossed aside
Just Kings and Queens in the midst of another game of Chess.

Choices: A Sonnet

Two lines of blue appear on white plastic.
Should I feel sad? Or enthusiastic?
My body feels like foreign territory,
In conquest sycophants scream of new-found
glory.
"Mother" is not who I wanted to be…
Someone I don't know made that choice for me.
They force me down and make me yield control
My stomach wretches and my eyes go dull
I gasp and cry until my vision's black
Decades of progress, in a day they throw me
back.
The men and traitors who sit in their pews
All black silken robes and their fresh-pressed
suits
Dictate their will on the battlefield of my body-
I never wanted this, but they made that choice
for me.

Clay Woman

There's a woman made from clay
She crumbles at the slightest sight of rain
I see her when I look for my own face
In the mirror

Her color has faded to gray
The paint around her eyes has chipped away
Cracked porcelain on full display
In my mirror.

Fade

I give
And give
And give again.

Then, when it's my turn to take, you fade
You fade away
You fade

Like mist in an invisible wind
Escaping with every careful word I crafted for
only you,
You go and fade,
Fade away

When the stars, Earth and moon don't orbit and
shine for only you
You fade away
You fade.

Fear

I sometimes wish my body could dissolve;
That I could claw away my skin and crawl inside
A hollow nest I built inside my chest.

I view my life through a distorted lens
From ten feet above where I stand

Slamming doors and hoarse voices
Make up a handful of the many noises
That balance me on a razor's edge

Tears ready to spill on demand
Rehearsed from a fear someone branded in my
skin.

Los Angeles

A friend turned acquaintance
Tells tales of their latest denim-clad heartbreak
Through confetti flames in a pit on the sand.

In the golden land where stars are born,
Beauties on silver screens made us think our
lives
Should be composed of so much more.

So we gather around a fire near the ocean,
Holding on to promises made;

A jewel encrusted life that's out of reach-
While plastic bags and aluminum cans wash
ashore on the beach.

Nostalgia

His voice comes through the stereo
While I drive alone at night in San Diego,
Sounding like someone I could have loved in
another life

A guitar hums low under traffic lights
It may be a song I know, or knew
At the sound, polaroid pictures flash behind my
eyes;

City Lights
Indie Tracks
Coastal Nights

Nostalgia for the things I never had
As I speed down the highway
To the soundtrack of a life I'll never live.

Parade

An ensemble of skeletons dance around my closet
Ghosts of dusty bones recite me tired sonnets
All the shame I own in a glittering parade
Day by day,
I march to the pounding drums of my own mistakes

Power

Never will it fail to amaze
That handfuls of men in fortified towers
Hiding like cowards behind ivory gates
Know the strings to pull, things to say,
To make brother slaughter brother,
Sister deceive sister,
Setting towns ablaze
Fire consuming fire
While they hide away.

Preacher Man

Practice what you preach, preacher man
Before you ascend to the promised land

Hypocrisy makes a frantic devil dance
Practice what you preach, preacher man

Misread pages birth a righteous wolf
That stalks its prey from behind oaken pews

Until false modesty poisons the flock,
And the sheep become wolves too

So run while you can
Run, run, run preacher man.

Pride

If I must hit the ground
I insist I do so covered in bruises
With a broken bone or two

If I must go somewhere
Even though I've adamantly refused,
I'll cross that bridge then burn it too.

The saying goes:
"Damn your Pride, I'd rather be happy than
dignified"

But I don't know how to be happy without my
pride-
What am I if not dignified?

Shell

This ghost of myself
Still haunts its hollow shell

Her nails scrape paint from outside my door
While I cower under damp sheets

In the dead of night her dead eyes glow
From the black space beneath my bed

I cover mirrors, and sleep with the lights on
To avoid the sight of this mournful apparition

Still, she makes her presence known
In the echo of moans and sorrowful shrieking

This ghost of myself
Will haunt me until she's back inside her shell.

Smoke

I found myself in puffs of smoke
Wafting between broken bookshelves
I saw myself for the first time
In the reflection of eyes I didn't know
Beneath a string of Christmas lights
As my lungs exhaled the sweet but bitter smoke.

Tattoo

He gave me a tattoo of blooming purple and blue
Even as his lustful handprint fades
My fear of being seen and touched,
Or alone at night,
Remains.

The Crowd

Yesterday I saw someone bleeding in the street
No one stopped to help
Instead the crowd merely screamed

"What about me? What about what I need?"

That someone bled out,
People walked on by-
As they passed, their shoes left scarlet footprints
behind

Temporary

A balmy night in summer, drunk with pride
It took us two hours to stumble to the beach
Fireworks in glowing bursts of blue and green
Lit a clear night sky, igniting from behind palm
trees

We tried to make our phones catch the
moonlight
Shining off the sea
Her majesty diminished to a weak silver speck
Reflecting off a neon screen

The photo never came out right
The reason, I think
Is that this feeling might
Be meant to be temporary.

www.ingramcontent.com/pod-product-compliance
Lightning Source LLC
Chambersburg PA
CBHW062110140826
49812CB00058B/1225
* 9 7 8 9 3 9 5 9 5 0 4 0 4 *